ATLANTA
MOTOR SPEEDWAY
A
Weekend
at the Track

by Kathy Persinger

SP
SPORTS PUBLISHING L.L.C.

www.SportsPublishingLLC.com

Publisher: **Peter L. Bannon**

Director of Production: **Susan M. Moyer**

Art Director: **K. Jeffrey Higgerson**

Developmental Editor: **Lynnette A. Bogard**

Senior Graphic Designer: **Kenneth J. O'Brien**

Copy Editor: **Cynthia L. McNew**

Dust Jacket Design: **Joseph Brumleve**

Printed in the United States of America.

ISBN: 1-58261-663-9

Sports Publishing L.L.C.
www.sportspublishingllc.com

ATLANTA

ATLANTA

ACKNOWLEDGMENTS

When Ed Clark was a youngster of about eight or nine growing up in Virginia, his Uncle Barry took him to a race. Martinsville was nearby, and it seemed like the thing to do. Mr. Clark had shown years before that he was quite good at racing a tricycle, so when he eventually got to see the real thing—even visit the pits, when he was too young to do so—it left a lasting desire in him to become part of it all.

Mr. Clark, the president and general manager of Atlanta Motor Speedway, still has his program from that first race.

I'd like to thank him for being a part of this book and for sharing his passion for the sport, his knowledge and his visions for the future of NASCAR.

Thank you to Angela Clare and Cheryl Hamilton of the speedway's public relations department, for their friendly guidance and willingness to help.

And thanks to the staff of the Hampton, Georgia, Chamber of Commerce for information about their city.

And of course, thanks to Lynnette Bogard and the crew at Sports Publishing, who gave me this opportunity.

Indirectly, I'd like to thank H.A. "Humpy" Wheeler, the president and general manager of Lowe's Motor Speedway near Charlotte, North Carolina. His influence on the sport of auto racing and his methods for making it a nationwide success were, and are, a powerful influence on Mr. Clark, a former Lowe's employee and a devoted student of Mr. Wheeler.

Finally, I'd like to thank my children—Christopher, Sarah and Tyler—for their love, their support and their ever-growing interest in watching cars speed through left turns on Sunday afternoons.

Table of Contents

Photo/Tom Copeland

INTRODUCTION

There is a small playground in the middle of the infield, the quick-setup kind with a carpet of artificial grass, a slide and things to climb on. It is connected to a tent put up by Motor Racing Outreach. Three children jump and play inside the chain-link fence with a beach ball. The wind is calm; the ball doesn't leave the make-believe yard.

Across the paved path, a retired school bus, labeled the NASBUS, supports a crowd of fans standing on its roof.

Next to the bus, in front of a motor home, two women sit in lawn chairs, talking. At the two souvenir trailers a few yards away, the salesmen lean on their counters and watch the children with the beach ball. It's Sunday afternoon, midway through the Bass Pro Shops/MBNA 500 race at Atlanta Motor Speedway, and nobody's shopping.

Here in the center of the 120-acre infield, the roar of the cars is more of a purr. People can speak without screaming. You can hear the children's laughter.

Of course, relaxation here is a fan thing. Since being redesigned in 1997, Atlanta Motor Speedway in Hampton, Georgia, has produced faster speeds than Daytona. Faster than Talladega. When the 1.54-mile quad-oval track was reconfigured, the backstretch became the frontstretch, creating wider areas in all four turns, allowing drivers to maintain speed in the corners.

Relaxation is not a driver thing.

"Not-so-fast turns into really fast in a heartbeat," Kyle Petty once said. "Just somebody slowing to pit and forgetting to give a hand signal can lead to a pileup at Atlanta, because you catch them so quick."

On this day, though, there aren't any pileups.

On this day, the track's 124,000 seats are nearly full, the infield is packed, and cars are parked on curbs for miles around the perimeter, waiting for the traffic jam that will inch along after the race on Highways 19 & 41 and, eventually, I-75.

This book takes a look at Atlanta Motor Speedway, the facility, the people who make it work, and the drivers who try to tame it.

This is a day in Hampton, Georgia, 30228. Let's ride.

CHAPTER

One Town
to the Right

Atlanta Motor Speedway is not in Atlanta, Georgia, but in Hampton, on a spread of about 870 acres 20 miles southeast of its namesake city.

From its inception in 1958, the track has changed as much as the Southern landscape surrounding it. In the beginning, a group of men—Walker Jackson, Lloyd Smith, Garland Bagley, Ralph Sceiano and Ike Supporter—decided to build a superspeedway, but funding became a problem and the inaugural founders quit the project. Bagley corralled another group—men named Warren Gremmel, Bill Boyd, Jack Black and Art Lester—and together, they spent $1.8 million to get the track ready to race.

It would become the seventh superspeedway in the country—meaning it

Matt Kenseth is introduced at Atlanta Motor Speedway prior to the Bass Pro Shops/MBNA 500, March 9, 2003.

Photo/Harold Hinson

was more than a mile long and paved—to host what would become Winston Cup racing.

But when the 1.5-mile road, known then as Atlanta International Raceway, debuted on July 31, 1960, it was a mess. The lower seats were so low that fans couldn't see over the retaining wall. In the infield, the only restroom facility was a three-unit outhouse. The ground was muddy enough to prompt Furman Bisher, then a columnist for *The Atlanta Journal* and *Atlanta Constitution*, to write, "Talk about Mudville. Casey would have been right at home."

Money continued to be a burden in the 1960s and 1970s, and the track was reorganized under Chapter 10 bankruptcy proceedings. After shuffling though several general managers, Walt Nix took over in the 1970s and served

The traditional flyover that typically accompanies the conclusion of the national anthem.
Photo/David Bogard

much of two decades, save a brief period when NASCAR president Mike Helton filled the role.

But even with money such an issue, people still flocked to the track, including one United States president who took a liking to the place. When running for governor of Georgia, Jimmy Carter—who had worked as a ticket vendor at the track in the 1960s—promised to host a barbecue dinner at the governor's mansion if he won. He did that, then hosted another, at the White House in 1978, and invited the racing community to join in.

On October 23, 1990, Bruton Smith bought Atlanta International Raceway and looked around. There was one grandstand, the Weaver Grandstand, and fans would bring blankets and sit

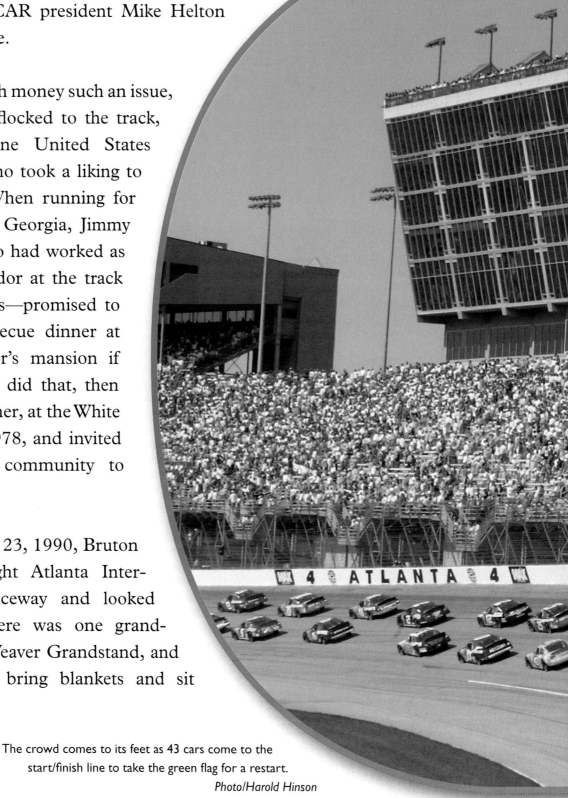

The crowd comes to its feet as 43 cars come to the start/finish line to take the green flag for a restart.
Photo/Harold Hinson

on the dirt banks. The bleachers were made of wood. This, Smith decided, would not be a player in the big game.

Smith changed the track's name to Atlanta Motor Speedway, constructed the East Turn Grandstand and increased the seating capacity to 25,000, with 30 luxury suites along the top. He brought in the Busch Series, the ARCA series, Indy races, and even dog shows.

In 1994, Tara Place, a nine-story building with 46 condominiums, opened, as did the Tara Ballroom and Tara Clubhouse, with its swimming pool and tennis courts. The next year, the North Turn Grandstand opened, then the Champions Grandstand, and the number of luxury suites was increased to 137.

Photo/Tom Copeland

When the Champions Grandstand was built, the start/finish line was moved from the west side to the east side of the track, making the route a 1.54-mile quad-oval. New media facilities and garages also were added.

Today, if you look back behind turn three, there is an old wooden building, a two-story structure, that sits on a hill overlooking progress like an uninvited guest. It resembles a press box at a country high school football game—painted white and red, the tiny building seems intimidated by the tall glass and steel structures along the fences elsewhere, where the money and the brass come to watch the races.

This is a building called Tower 3, a structure of about 80 feet by 80 feet, which houses four suites. It is the building in which team owner Rick Hendrick was sitting when he first saw Jeff Gordon race. "Jeff made an impression, and Rick wanted

Photo/Harold Hinson

Photo/Tom Copeland

Jeff to drive for him," says the track's Ed Clark. "From there, you're just right on the track, and he [Hendrick] could see Jeff's hands on the wheel and see how he was working the track."

Maybe, in a sport that is churning rapidly away from its roots, some things are worth keeping.

HAMPTON, GEORGIA
Henry County

Population (according to the 2000 census): 3,857
Named for: Confederate General Wade Hampton
Hot fact: Ranked No. 4 among nation's counties for rate of population growth in the 1990s at 103 percent.
Newspaper: *The Daily Herald*, which covers Henry County.
School districts: One
Number of schools: 28, including elementary, middle and high schools.

Photo/Tom Copeland

CHAPTER

2

Who's Running the Show

O. Bruton Smith: Track owner and Chief Executive Officer of Speedway Motorsports, Inc.

Atlanta Motor Speedway ticket manager Frances Goss has a memory of when Olin Bruton Smith decided to purchase this racetrack near Atlanta.

"Bruton told me before he ever bought the track, 'I'd like to see what could be done with this place,'" Goss once said. "He's made it. I never would have believed Atlanta Motor Speedway would look like it does today."

Smith, who grew up in tiny Oakboro, North Carolina, started his fascination with cars in the 1950s, when he became an automobile dealer and began promoting NASCAR events. He gained a reputation as a fair promoter who put fans' needs first at the tracks he leased around North Carolina.

In 1959, Smith built his first racetrack, Charlotte Motor Speedway, and hosted the first race there in June 1960. He also took on business interests in Texas and Illinois, worked at car dealerships, and became a Ford Motor Company executive.

In 1974, Smith founded Speedway Motorsports, Inc. and in 1975 made it the first motorsports company to be traded on the New York Stock Exchange. Today, SMI operates six tracks—Atlanta, Bristol Motor Speedway, Lowe's Motor Speedway (formerly Charlotte), Las Vegas Motor Speedway, Infineon Raceway (formerly Sears Point) and Texas Motor Speedway. SMI

O. Bruton Smith
Photo/Harold Hinson

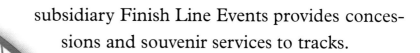

subsidiary Finish Line Events provides concessions and souvenir services to tracks.

In 1992, Smith was responsible for adding a lighting system to Lowe's Motor Speedway to make it the first track able to host a NASCAR race after dark.

In 1996, he was named to the Forbes 400 list as one of the wealthiest people in the United States.

In 1997, Smith organized his business interests as Sonic Automotive—which owns and operates more than 170 car dealerships and more than 30 collision centers across the country—and placed it on the New York Stock Exchange.

Smith also is the majority owner of a Class A baseball team, the Kan-

Jeff Burton waves to the crowd at driver introductions.
Photo/Harold Hinson

napolis (N.C.) Intimidators, named for Kannapolis native Dale Earnhardt. He founded Speedway Children's Charities in 1984, a non-profit organization that has raised more than $5 million.

In 1997, Smith was honored with the NASCAR Award of Excellence for his work with children's charities.

Ed Clark: President and General Manager

Ed Clark was born in December, 1954, in Keysville, Virginia, and has been with Atlanta Motor Speedway since 1992—but he has been around NASCAR for decades.

While a child still in elementary school, he fell in love with auto racing. "We usually would go to Martinsville," he says, "and for a

Bruton Smith, center, president of the Atlanta Motor Speedway, smiles as he hands House Speaker Rep. Terry Coleman, D-Eastman, right, a gavel in the House of Representatives with Atlanta Motor Speedway general manager, Ed Clark, left, during a tour of the Georgia House and Senate, Thursday, March 6, 2003, at the Capitol in Atlanta.

(Photo by AP/WWP)

week, I couldn't sleep. I had a bag full with a camera, an autograph book and film. It was always a very special time."

Clark covered the sport for his local newspaper during high school, going to Richmond and Martinsville before he was old enough to be given a pit pass. A school friend worked as the photographer. "We got some articles," he says. "They weren't the best; they weren't the worst."

He then went on to Virginia Tech, where he had a newspaper delivery route and wrote a Sunday column on auto racing. "It all kind of grew out of that," he says.

He got a degree in horticulture in 1977, but his big break with NASCAR tracks came at Bristol

Country and western singer Linda Davis sings the national anthem prior to the Bass Pro Shops/MBNA 500.
Photo/Harold Hinson

Motor Speedway, where he was hired a month before graduation and eventually became its public relations director.

Two years later, he went to Nashville Raceway as the track's general manager. In 1981, in his mid-20s, he moved to Charlotte Motor Speedway's public relations department.

He soon became public relations director and in 1987 was named vice president of events. Lowe's president and general manager H.A. "Humpy" Wheeler became a big influence in his life.

In 1992, Bruton Smith decided to give Clark a new role: He was recruited to direct the management team of Atlanta Motor Speedway and in 1995 was promoted to president of the track.

Photo/Tom Copeland

Today, Clark is executive vice president of the board of directors of Speedway Motorsports Inc., co-chairman of Speedway Children's Charities Foundation, a member of the National Council of the Boy Scouts of America and serves on the board of directors of the Atlanta Convention and Visitors' Bureau and Motor Racing Outreach. He is a former president of the Henry County Convention & Visitors' Bureau.

Clark and his wife of more than two decades, Teresa, have a daughter, Nicki, and son, Collin. They live in Peachtree City, Georgia.

Photo/Tom Copeland

Photo/Harold Hinson

CHAPTER

3

The
Road More
Traveled

The Winston Cup tour passes through Atlanta twice each season, but there's more to the speedway than stock car racing in March and October.

"Anything that has the name 'show' on it, we've had at some point," says track president and general manager Ed Clark. "The kennel club show is a huge annual event. There are music shows, a number of big concerts…"

In 1999, for example, the Hard Rock Cafe Rockfest brought in 100,000 people for a day.

The speedway counts its usage as more than 300 days a year, though each special event—an auto show, a music fest—is tabulated as one day.

Photo/Harold Hinson

"Those are each counted as a rental day," Clark says, "so it may be closer to 275 days a year."

Still....

There also are spectator tours that include a brief track history, a visit to the Petty Garden, a peek at the luxury suites and a stroll through the garages and Victory Lane. Tour participants also can go for a two-lap ride around the track in an official speedway van.

The Cup races—the Bass Pro Shops/MBNA 500 in March and the Georgia 500 in October—are the two largest single-day sports events in the state, and with its Busch and ARCA races, the Legends series and other events, the track

Photo/Harold Hinson

is projected to bring in more than $2.275 billion over five years to the Atlanta-area economy. Statisticians' projected intake from Atlanta's three major league teams—Major League Baseball's Atlanta Braves ($526 million), the National Football League's Atlanta Falcons ($48 million) and the National Basketball Association's Atlanta Hawks ($163 million)—are farther down the scale.

Throw in corporate events, car shows, driving schools, concerts and maybe a circus or two, and the speedway's "Closed" sign isn't up very often.

"If you think of someone like the Braves, people will come and spend their money, then go home," Clark says. "With us, people come and stay three or four days, and they spend their money at

Georgia native Mark Gibson celebrates his first win at AMS in the ARCA 400, March 8, 2003.

Photo/Harold Hinson

the hotels, in the restaurants. We're appreciated for the economy we bring to the state."

Gary Stoken, president of the Atlanta Sports Council, says in a statement, "Atlanta Motor Speedway is obviously responsible for a huge part of the sports business in this town. Race events bring people from all over the world to Atlanta, much more than the local teams and local events.

"When you look at attendance for just the two Winston Cup races, that's equivalent to filling up the Georgia Dome several times, just for a single race.

"The amount of attention Atlanta Motor Speedway attracts from people of every state and from all across the world is invaluable. In addition to the many race fans and media members who come to

Photo/Harold Hinson

Atlanta, there are millions more watching on TV. The Winston Cup and Indy races garner a tremendous amount of media, and that's the kind of attention you can't pay for."

While national recognition is priceless, there's an aspect of local involvement that track president Ed Clark, who concerns himself daily with promoting the track's presence and spirit toward the area, considers just as special.

"I'm on a lot of boards... I'm the past president of the Chamber of Commerce, I'm on the board of directors of the Flint River Scout Council, I'm on the board of the Atlanta Convention & Visitors Bureau..." he says. "It's a great networking opportunity. But being on the board of Speedway Children's Charities, it's one of the most heartwarming things.

Photo/Harold Hinson

"It is one of the things about my job that is the most rewarding of all."

The Christmas party, for that charity, is the key.

"We have them [the children's organizations that are recipients of the funds] all out for a Christmas party, and they're so innocent and so pure, and I get more out of that than anything I do. We give back to 30 or 35 organizations a year, and when we can help, we certainly want to do that.

"Part of the obligation you've got is being part of the community."

Photo/Harold Hinson

Based on the 2003 schedules, this is a typical race year at Atlanta Motor Speedway.

Speedway schedule:

March 7: Georgia Power qualifying day

March 8: ARCA 400

March 9: Bass Pro Shops MBNA 500 Winston Cup race

September 20: NOPI Nationals Motorsports Supershow

October 24: Goody's Dash 150 and Georgia-Pacific qualifying night

October 25: Aaron's 312 Busch race

October 26: Georgia 500 Winston Cup race

Legends schedule:

April 12: Legends, Bandolero and Thunder Roadster quarter-mile events

June 5: Thursday Thunder racing

June 12: Thursday Thunder racing

June 19: Thursday Thunder racing

June 26: Thursday Thunder racing

July 3: Thursday Thunder racing

July 10: Thursday Thunder racing

July 17: Thursday Thunder racing

July 24: Thursday Thunder racing

July 31: Thursday Thunder racing

August 7: Thursday Thunder racing

October 3: Legends, Bandolero and Thunder Roadster quarter-mile events

November 7: Legends, Bandolero and Thunder Roadster quarter-mile events

Mark Martin's coach driver, Randy, polishes Mark's coach.
Photo/Terry Renna

CHAPTER

4

A Day
at the Races

Before the fans even think about coming, before the tickets are printed and the first load of popcorn is ordered, the staff and crew at Atlanta Motor Speedway are preparing.

When you're going to host a party for more than 150,000 people, you don't procrastinate.

"One thing I will tell you is, if we were doing this for the first time, I couldn't even imagine the preparation and all it would take," says speedway president Ed Clark.

Clark knows. He's been doing this most of his life.

The crowd had barely cleared from the Bass Pro Shops/ MBNA 500 March 2003 race, for example, and he was well into planning the next gig.

Photo/Harold Hinson

"It's an ongoing process," he says. "Like right now, we're working on October [the Georgia 500] and next March. And on some aspects of things, even beyond that."

Following a race, the track staff gets a few days off. Down time, time to relax and tread water before riding the next wave.

"Certainly after a race, we've got to take a couple of days, days for cleaning things up and taking a long weekend, but then we're head first into the next event," Clark says. Atlanta Motor Speedway has a full-time staff of 63 people. During a race event, that number swells to about 5,000. Some are volunteers, some are specialists.

"Fortunately, we have a lot of key employees and a lot of key people who can supervise," Clark says. "The

Photo/Harold Hinson

guy who oversees the parking in the infield, he has been doing that for many, many years. He knows the things they need to get assistance with.

"And we've got so many people who are in the same scenario."

The intense portion of planning starts several months before a race.

There are briefing meetings with the traffic crew, the people who will help park the cars, the suite workers, the security personnel.

"It's where we walk through the game plan," Clark says. "We critique the last event, we have a prevention coordination meeting [to deal with any problems that previously occurred], then after the race, we'll

Photo/Harold Hinson

have a postrace critique and talk about any more possible solutions."

As much as they put into it, there's always something that happens that advance planning won't solve. But that's to be expected when you're adding so many people to a town that only has about 3,800 residents.

"Everything that can happen in a [race property] 'city' of that size ... we've had it happen," Clark says. "We've had people die. We've had babies born. And every situation in between. You just have to prepare and try to take care of it."

During race week, from Tuesday until the last car and motor home are out on Sunday or Monday, the track is open and operating 24 hours a day. Campers can begin arriving up to 10 days ahead of time,

Photo/Harold Hinson

and the parking attendants, camping organizers and security officers already are on the job.

But for all that happens backstage, for all the mind-bending work put into these performances, Clark says he hardly ever sees a race. At least not much of one.

He describes a typical race day for him by using a phrase coined by Lowe's Motor Speedway president H.A. "Humpy" Wheeler: "Tickets, traffic and toilets."

"Boy, there's so much to it," Clark says. "On a typical day, gates open at eight o'clock, and we use a lot of civic groups to run the concessions and souvenirs. So I have to have everyone in place. Then there are the prerace activities. I generally will have a few meetings on race morning. Then I try to make the drivers' meeting and go down and check all that out before the race.

Photo/David Bogard

"Then I come up to the control tower before the start and make sure the traffic is in and there are no problems around the facility. Then I'll go out and check the cleanup and the restrooms and things like that."

While the race is zipping past outside, there's so much to be taken care of inside.

"I go see sponsors and talk to people involved," Clark says. "Then I go to Victory Lane, and then I go up in a helicopter and watch traffic and see how things are going. Then I go home and have the best sleep I've had in ages."

That part about traffic can be enough to turn sleep into nightmares. The speedway is approximately eight miles from I-75, the main highway through Atlanta. But with help from the Department of Transportation and State

The dreaded jet dryers—an unwelcome sight at any race weekend.
Photo/Nicole Nance

Highway Patrol, the track is finding ways to help fans leave easier.

"That's something that's been a problem since the track was built," Clark says. "But it's a lot better than it was. Even better news is that State Road 20 [a four-lane highway extension with a direct link to I-75] should be finished by spring 2005. It'll go right from the back grandstand to the interstate, and that should improve exit time by about 40 percent."

For everyone wanting to leave on a Sunday afternoon, it takes about three and a half hours. "That's last car out. A lot of people want to sit around and tailgate for a while," Clark says.

Recently, the Department of Transportation changed the traffic pattern to so that some vehicles had to travel south before going north, to improve the flow.

Photo/David Bogard

"The interesting thing is we ended up getting more compliments than complaints. And I can't ever remember that happening," Clark says.

But what about the race, the one he hosted and never saw?

It happens, eventually.

"I get a tape about a month later," he says. "I pop some popcorn and watch it."

Waiting in the infield in turn four for the roar of 43 engines and the smell of octane and rubber.
Photo/Richard Hill

CHAPTER

5

Just
the Facts

S ometimes numbers can come up in intriguing ways.

On November 12, 1995, the late Dale Earnhardt, driving the No. 3 car, set a 500-mile race record at Atlanta Motor Speedway. His average speed was 163.633 miles per hour.

The time of the race was three hours, three minutes and three seconds.

Courtesy of the speedway's public relations department, here are other basic statistics about the track.

Constructed: 1959-1960; reconfiguration completed in November, 1997.

First race: July 31, 1960 (the Dixie 200).

Photo/Harold Hinson

First race winner: Fireball Roberts.

First race pole: Fireball Roberts (four-lap average speed: 133.870).

Track location: 20 miles south of Atlanta, Georgia, on Highways 19 & 41.

Property: 870 acres.

The track: 1.54-mile quad-oval.

Racing surface: 55-60 feet wide.

Turns: Approximately one-quarter mile, banked 24 degrees.

Straightaways: Banked five degrees.

Length of frontstretch, including dogleg: 2,332 feet.

Tara Place.
Photo/Harold Hinson

Length of backstretch: 1,800 feet.

Pit road: 1,320 feet.

Infield: Approximately 120 acres.

OTHER RECORDS:

One-lap qualifying record for NASCAR Winston Cup: Geoffrey Bodine, 197.478 mph, 28.074 seconds. Set November 15, 1997.

Indy Racing League record: Billy Boat, 224.145 mph, 24.734 seconds. Set August 28, 1998.

FEATURES:

Tara Place Condominiums: Forty-six luxury condos opened above the Richard Petty Grandstand in November, 1994, with two- and

Photo/Harold Hinson

three-bedroom units and stadium-style seating. The building also has a clubhouse, swimming pool, tennis courts and fitness room. The nine-story building houses the track's corporate offices and has a ballroom, exhibition hall and banquet facility.

Petty Garden: Located in front of the gift shop and ticket office, the garden has a seven-foot statue of racing legend Richard Petty signing an autograph for a young fan.

Gift Shop: The shop, next to Tara Place, sells everything from T-shirts and other clothing to driver souvenirs and speedway memorabilia.

Message Center: A four-color message center at the speedway's main entrance allows drivers to display messages to fans and visitors.

Michael Waltrip practices his swing in the driver's lot in the infield.
Photo/Terry Nance

Track tours: Available daily and running every half-hour during operating hours, Monday through Saturday 9 a.m. to 4:30 p.m. and Sundays 1 p.m. to 4:30 p.m. Cost is $5 for adults, $3 for children, and free for those six and younger. Call (770) 707-7970.

Luxury suites: There are 141 of them, some of which can be used to entertain up to 68 people.

RACING EVENTS

Georgia Power Qualifying Day: Winston Cup qualifying the Friday before the spring race.

ARCA 400: The Saturday before the spring Winston Cup race.

Bass Pro Shops/MBNA 500: The spring Winston Cup race. Top finishes include Dale Earnhardt edging Bobby Labonte by .01 seconds in 2000 for his ninth win at Atlanta.

Photo/Terry Nance

NOPI Nationals: About 70,000 people come to this two-day event, which showcases more than 5,000 show cars and trucks in 300 classes. Cash and prizes exceed $100,000.

Georgia-Pacific Qualifying Night: Winston Cup qualifying night for the October race.

Aaron's 312 Busch Race: The longest Busch race of the season, held the Saturday before the fall Cup race.

Georgia 500: Spectators have come from all 50 states and a dozen foreign countries for the October Winston Cup event.

Legends Thursday Thunder Summer Series: A 10-week summer series for Legends cars, Bandoleros and Roadsters racing in nine classes.

BET YOU DIDN'T KNOW...

- On a typical race day, fans consume 11,750 hamburgers and hot dogs—enough to feed a family of four three meals a day for three years.

- Race fans also go through 150 cases of toilet paper on a typical race day, each package containing six jumbo rolls. That's 340 miles of toilet paper, enough to circle the track 221 times.

- Fans will consume 1,040 cases of beer at a race, enough to provide every household in Hampton, Georgia, with a case and still have 56 remaining.

- You could fit 79 Georgia Domes on Atlanta Motor Speedway's property.

- In the infield, you could fit 11 Georgia Domes or 19 aircraft carriers.

Michael Waltrip gets a kiss from his daughter Macy for good luck.
Photo/Harold Hinson

CHAPTER

6

Speaking of Atlanta...

When Atlanta Motor Speedway was redesigned in 1997, the turns were widened, which led to increased speeds in the corners. It's a fast track, and drivers know there isn't a lot of need to hit the brakes. Here's what some of them have to say.

"Every time you blink, you've gone a football field. Sneeze, and you've missed the backstretch. Everything just happens so fast there."
—Kyle Petty

"It's a very non-forgiving racetrack. It's a track where there is a fine line on missing the setup. You end up with a sort of love-hate thing. If you miss it big-time, it can be pretty embarrassing."
—Ricky Rudd

Sterling Marlin
Photo/David Bogard

"This is one of the tracks that I like to go fast at and like to go good at. When you get the car handling right, it just makes it a lot more fun."

—Bobby Labonte

"Even though aero[dynamics] is a big issue there, the track widens out quite a bit. Twenty laps into a run, you've got guys who will run right down on the line on the bottom of the track and you've got guys who will run clear up by the wall. It's a track that gives you the kind of flexibility that we have at Michigan, to where however your car is driving, you can move around on the racetrack and find a spot that helps you and your car not be so aero-sensitive."

—Tony Stewart

Jeff Gordon
Photo/David Bogard

"This may only be a one and a half-mile track in distance, but it races like a superspeedway, and those are the types of tracks we seem most comfortable running."
—Chad Little

"Atlanta Motor Speedway is one of my favorite tracks and a track that we've had some success on. It offers multi-groove racing, which allows for more passing, and in my opinion, better racing. Tracks with multiple grooves really work in my favor because with my dirt background, I keep searching around for a line that works and usually find something before the day is over."
—Jimmie Johnson

Jimmie Johnson
Photo/David Bogard

"Atlanta is great. It's no secret that the faster it is, the better I like it. ... The multi-groove deal means it puts a lot into the hands of the driver. If you're not getting it done in the low groove, you can move the car around to find a line that works for the setup."

—Dale Earnhardt Jr.

"Atlanta, because it is so quick, you can't bobble at all, because your corner speed is almost the same as your straightaway speed. ... Atlanta is just really a fast track. It's the entry to the corners and the way the track is laid out that allow it."

—John Andretti

Sterling Marlin
Photo/David Bogard

"I really like Atlanta and always have. Atlanta is one of the fastest unrestricted tracks we race on, so I'm always excited to go there. Atlanta is high-banked and fast—I really like it because of the banking. You can get some major speed off the corners onto the straights."
—Matt Kenseth

"There are a few tracks that I've always struggled on, and that's the bigger, banked tracks like Atlanta. It's not that I haven't done well there. My first Busch race I went from a provisional to leading the race. ... We just haven't had the track record there that we've wanted."
—Casey Atwood

"I always run better at tracks like Atlanta."
**—Mark Dismore,
Indy Racing League**

Tony Stewart
Photo/David Bogard

"Atlanta hasn't been one of my favorite tracks since they reconfigured it a few years ago, but the racing has gotten better every time we go to the track. Over the past few years, the groove has widened, and we have seen some really exciting racing with a lot of passing and lead changes."

—Ken Schrader

"Historically, Atlanta hasn't been the best track for me. I've had solid finishes there, but I haven't had the top five finishes that I want. ... The key to success at Atlanta is being able to change with the track. As the race goes on, the groove gets higher. You have to have a car that can adapt with the track changes."

—Kenny Wallace

Kevin Harvick
Photo/David Bogard

"The old Atlanta had a personality about it, the way the corners were banked. When they came back and redid it, they banked the lower corner a little bit more, and it became a little bit quicker. The old speedway, it was less banked at the bottom, and you could gain a little bit more at the top. ... I really enjoyed the old track. It had a personality of its own."
—Bill Elliott

"I like the track, and I have had some pretty good runs there. I go around the race-track and actually try to decipher what the car is doing, where it's doing it at, and come back and relay the message to the crew. ... The good thing about it, we make our decisions based on a lot of engineering facts and the group-type decision-making process. It really makes it easier on all of us."
—Jeremy Mayfield

Matt Kenseth
Photo/David Bogard

"For such a long time, Atlanta was the championship place. A lot of those championship battles came down to the last race of the year, and Atlanta was that race for a long time. ... The funny thing is, Atlanta still plays a huge role in deciding the championship. All races do. The March race at Atlanta and the October race at Atlanta, no difference. It's the same number of points, and the race can help you or hurt you just as much."
—Kyle Petty

"I like to win races, and I like to win championships, but just being around here has always been fun—ever since I was a little kid."
—Dale Earnhardt Jr.

Jeff Gordon
Photo/David Bogard

111

"Atlanta is a great race facility. Every one of Bruton Smith's tracks is first-class. Atlanta is like Daytona for the Winston Cup drivers—it's relatively easy to drive flat by yourself, but in a pack, if you lose the draft, you're done. Likewise, if you don't know how to work the draft, you can catch up to a lot of people. It's very aggressive racing, which I enjoy."

**—Eddie Cheever Jr.,
Indy Racing League**

"I like racing at Atlanta Motor Speedway. The track is very much like Texas, but Atlanta is a much better track to race on. It is much smoother and also wider, so it gives you more room to maneuver and pass. The track lights at Atlanta Motor Speedway are fantastic, and you can see clearly around the whole track. I like the whole facility, and the people down there as well."

**—Stephan Gregoire,
Indy Racing League**

Sterling Marlin
Photo/David Bogard

More infield fans celebrating race day in turn four.
Photo/David Bogard

CHAPTER

7

The
Last Lap

When NASCAR racing first began to build its fan base, million-dollar payoffs, luxury suites and coast-to-coast marketing were unheard of.

But what started in June 1949, when the first sedans rolled around a track in Charlotte, North Carolina, in the inaugural organized stock car race has become big business worldwide.

Ask Ed Clark if he sometimes thinks the simpler days were better, when guys could build their own cars in back-yard garages and sponsorship money wasn't a necessity, and the Atlanta track president will vote on the side of progress.

"I told Humpy [Wheeler, of Lowe's Motor Speedway] many years ago

The pranksters of Billy Bad Ass Racing show their ability to tolerate the chilly conditions in early March. The temps that morning were in the upper 40s.

Photo/Terry Nance

Photo/David Bogard

that the day will come when every car has an in-car camera," he says. "And that's almost a reality now." Forward momentum, at a rapid pace.

"Change—I think that's a sign of progress," he says. "We have, well, I don't want to say it's a necessary part, but some of the areas have gotten so so-phisticated, that to go back to the basics might cut costs, but it would make us go backward."

Memories of the early years give way to towering grandstands and television contracts.

"You hear from fans that that was the good ol' days. But you can't go back," Clark says. "I think the sport is definitely healthy, and they [early drivers]built the foundation for what we're doing. I don't think we ought to think about going back. Those who long for the old days, well, I think we're doing better than the old days."

He says that for all the success Atlanta Motor Speedway has had, with fan and driver support and the track's economic impact on the city and the state, it's still an issue, in this changing occupation, to stay on top.

"There's a lot of challenge here at Atlanta. It's not an easy, automatic type of market. There are a lot of other entertainment things people can do," he says. "I've had the opportunity to go work at other speedways, but I've chosen to stay here. And it's because of the challenge of it.

"There's still a lot of growth here. This is my 25th year [working at race-tracks], and I can't wait to see what the next 25 will hold."

What might happen in the next 25 years?

"I think we may be running multiple events on the same day," he predicts. "I think we're truly going to become a national sport. We need more diversity, and that will come with time. But we've got people who are middle America, who work day in and day out to buy a ticket to come to this race, and we need to keep that in mind, too."

Forward momentum, with memories.

"It's such a pure sport that when it gets a hold on people, it won't let go. We have a long way to go, and we still have to figure that out. Every day."

Michael "Fatback" McSwain (crew chief for Bobby Labonte, who would go on to win the Bass Pro Shops/MBNA 500 the next day) poses for a picture in the infield on March 8th, 2003.
Photo/David Bogard

Photo/Nicole Nance

Photo/Harold Hinson

Celebrate the Heroes of Stock Car Racing
in These Other Acclaimed Titles from Sports Publishing

Matt Kenseth:
Above and Beyond
by Kelley Maruszewski
(Matt Kenseth's sister)

- 10 x 10 hardcover
- 160 pages
- color photos throughout
- $24.95
- 2003 release!

StockcarToons 2:
More Grins and Spins on the
Winston Cup Circuit
by Mike Smith, editorial cartoonist
for the *Las Vegas Sun*

- 11 x 8.5 softcover • 160 pages
- cartoons throughout
- $12.95 • 2003 release!

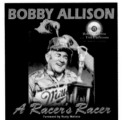

Bobby Allison:
A Racer's Racer
by Bobby Allison with
Tim Packman

- 10 x 10 hardcover
- 160 pages
- color photos throughout
- Includes an audio CD!
- $29.95
- 2003 release!

Tony Stewart:
High Octane in the Fast Lane
by The Associated Press
and AP/Wide World Photos

- 10 x 10 hardcover • 160 pages
- color photos throughout
- Includes a 60-minute audio CD!
- $39.95
- 2003 release!

Lowe's Motor Speedway:
A Weekend at the Track
by Kathy Persinger

- 8.5 x 11 hardcover
- 128 pages
- color photos throughout
- $24.95
- 2003 release!

As They Head for the Checkers:
Fantastic Finishes, Memorable Milestones and
Heroes Remembered from the World of Racing
by Kathy Persinger & Mark Garrow (audio)

- 10 x 10 hardcover • 160 pages
- 100 color and b/w photos throughout
- Includes an audio CD!
- $39.95
- 2003 release!

Along for the Ride
by Larry Woody

- 5.5 x 8 1/4 hardcover
- 191 pages
- photos throughout
- $19.95
- 2003 release!

Sterling Marlin: The Silver Bullet
by Larry Woody

- 8.5 x 11 hardcover • 128 pages
- 100 color photos throughout
- Includes a cdracecard CD-ROM!
- $29.95

Dale Earnhardt Jr.: Out of
the Shadow of Greatness
by Mike Hembree

- 10 x 10 hardcover
- 160 pages
- color photos throughout
- Includes a 60-minute audio CD!
- $39.95 • 2003 release!

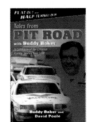

Flat Out and Half Turned
Over: Tales from Pit Road
with Buddy Baker
by Buddy Baker with David Poole

- 5.5 x 8.25 hardcover
- 169 pages
- photos throughout
- $19.95

Jeff Gordon:
Burning Up the Track
by the Indianapolis Star

- 10 x 10 hardcover
- 160 pages
- color photos throughout
- Includes a 60-minute audio CD!
- $39.95
- 2003 release!

The History of America's Greatest
Stock Car Tracks: From Daytona
to the Brickyard
by Kathy Persinger

- Oversized hardcover in the shape of
  a racetrack • 160 pages
- 100 color and b/w photos throughout
- $29.95

To order at any time, please call toll-free **1-877-424-BOOK (2665)**.
For fast service and quick delivery, order on-line at **www.SportsPublishingLLC.com**.